Projection

Projection

New Terminology Based on a Dual
System Derived from the Chinese Book
of Changes and Applied to Psychological
Considerations of Self, Action and Influence

James P. Devaney

Library of Congress Control Number: 2011907839
ISBN: Hardcover   978-1-4628-7367-8
                    Softcover   978-1-4628-7366-1
                    Ebook   978-1-4628-7368-5

To order additional copies of this book, contact:
Xlibris Corporation
1-888-795-4274
www.Xlibris.com
Orders@Xlibris.com
99638

For my Father (RIP)
And for my Mother, God Bless Her
For Monsignor Professor Michael Nolan (RIP)
For my Wife Jenny and our two sons Lenny and Tom
And for all those people, standing there, waiting.
Thank You.

CONTENTS

Projection

New Terminology Based on a Dual System Derived from the Chinese
Book of Changes and Applied to Psychological Considerations of Self,
Action and Influence

FOREWORD

ONE OF THE main points of arguments in the debate on the origin of language is "language is essential for thought".* However, now the viewpoint is being considered "thought is essential for communication".

So, while the philologists of the nineteenth century and modern linguists may wonder about the origins of language and attempt a simultaneous better understanding of thought, here, in what hopefully is more the purely psychological approach, thought is approached directly.

This direct approach certainly leaves the researcher more exposed to abysmal mistake. Here, a system of interdependent structures is put forward, all hinging on a general correctness. When as here new terminology is employed in an attempt to further highlight what old terminology there is which perhaps is not fully appreciated or understood (e.g. projection, idea, field, action); whether consciousness is structural or not, or maybe both structural and non-structural at once; or whether a structural description of consciousness is permissible or not. One's starting point is philosophical or metaphysical and one has already proceeded a long way on one's own without much criticism, and perhaps this is not a good thing.

Here, what has developed is a regard for thought as practically equivalent to sensory awareness, while not denying thought to be much more than this too. This view certainly is in harmony with contemporary empirical research philosophy.

Two more specific points for discussion are mentioned. Here, the whole location for mental activity is equated with social interaction. Denying the importance of the biological, physiological activity occurring within the

---

* "The Origin of Language: Aspects of the Discussion from Condillac to Wundt", by G.A.Wells, 1987. Wells is or was Professor of German at Birbeck College, University of London. There is some discussion in this book, relating gesture to the origin of language.

organism must be as bad a mistake as the more common one, which is here countered, of failing to recognize that to a limiting extent what takes place outside of the "boundary" of the organism is a part of the organism; deterministically and essentially linked to the doer.

The other point regards time and temporality, and the unlikeliness of anyone saying anything new about time. Yet, in a psychological sense it may not be too hard to accept that consciousness has some prerogative regarding time, in comparison to what is not conscious or inanimate. If that seems like such a reasonable statement, then what is the specific prerogative? Perhaps it underlies everything that we would define as intellectual or social in the human.

INTRODUCTION

THOUGHT AS DETERMINED by inter-individual relations—more, the possibility, by means of creative thought, of permitting, at least facilitating, action as an aspect of inter-individual relations, is considered.

As a demonstration of how action, seen here as an inter-individual bond, may be directly related to the thought interactivity among individuals, consider in a general manner those individuals described as developmentally disabled, mental deficient, autistically or psychotically affected. Not alone is such individuals, but perhaps reliably so with such, may be found a particular, characteristic attitude, especially evident towards or in response to any overt approach to these individuals; that is, to defer, in the extreme, to any approach; to put themselves beyond reach, as inaccessible as possible.

While realizing that mental deficiency, identified as such, ought not to be acknowledged as other than deficit; in a neutral sense, not claiming superiority but not denying all possibility of positivity, "emptiness" is the term used to refer to that condition of mind, which loosely speaking is the ideal one when it comes to the often delicate balancing with regard to action and idea in inter-individual relations.

Of course, this could be a compensatory development on the part of anyone with a handicap, and so it is not necessary to claim emptiness is a primary virtue.

If it is the emptiness, the lack of reactive responsiveness maintained by the individual that leads to a reaction in turn, or a coming-to-ahead of all reactions of relative individuals, that may lead to trouble for the emptying/emptied individuals; such as institutionalization, attempts at isolation, ostracization; it is that society will not forever tolerate one that does not permit a "certain something", this something to be described or posited here as the aimless scratching, moving, shifting, lack of stillness, form production of a body.

Note that it is not meant to be critical of society for the intolerance of those in its midst that persist, insist or persevere with their failing. Rather, it is intended to try to justify the fact of the intolerance.

Field is used in a new sense here, to refer to that which the abovementioned individuals, not all of whom, but some of whom, are relating otherwise arbitrary distinctions of action.

Ambivalent form is the term put forward to try to explain what the "form production" in question is: that rather aimless (it might be considered) activity all healthy individuals engage in at some time or another—namely, doing something of which they are not perfectly aware.

But to start at the beginning, something is to be said regarding the principles on which all that follows is based. The secondary principle (like the yin or dark principle of oriental philosophy) is considered as additive in nature: that is secondary-with-secondary (as 1 + 1). The primary is thought of as associative in nature (as in a grouping of the primary like 1 * 1 * 1 * 1 * . . . etc., where * indicates something like multiplication).

A combination of the primary with the secondary is more difficult to understand. In attempting to keep things simple, for example with projection, a primary-secondary unit is added, and this allows the structure of projection to be considered as broken up into two smaller structures (see Fig. 1). This is about as complex as the discussion gets regarding interaction of the principles.

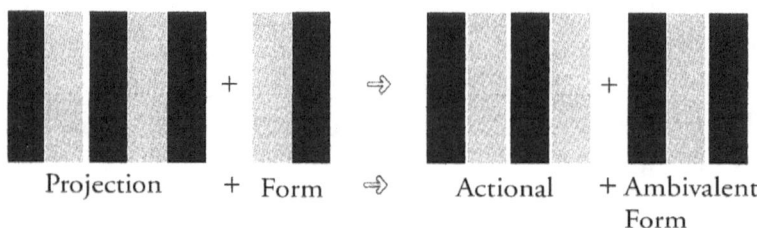

Projection   + Form   ⇨   Actional   + Ambivalent Form

Figure 1. Projection plus form results in actional plus ambivalent form.

For long there has been an interest in action, deriving no doubt from two years of Transcendental Meditation (1974-'76). Not just the specific teaching there, but associating with people some of whom had a practical understanding of yoga, led to this peculiar sense regarding action.

One of the first footnotes (which is actually an appendix to the book, it is so long) in the Maharishi Mahesh Yogi's translation of the first chapters of the Baghavad Gita was for this writer extremely hard to absorb. It is not that the reasoning is foreign in nature or style, but that it is so demanding. This book is important to mention, for though the writer is a very poor scholar yet regarding that area of study, it was covered superficially, and it is likely that the resolution of trinity with duality (with some help from the quaternity) which is used in explaining self-exterior / self-interior relations; the social vs. individual condition; and, unity and separation: results from identifying a process that has occurred in the writer perhaps twice if not more, and associating its occurrence with the famous injunction of that ancient Indian work "Be without the three Gunas", Krishna to Arjuna before the battle between the forces of light and darkness.

Not to leave any mystery, if possible, it is briefly stated that: awareness of what is volitional, at a special moment, if perceived (if one can use this term) as, one, a knocking on one's very own world, from without, and two, at the same time another knocking, from without on that same world, these knocks incongruously corresponding with the mundane chance knocking and banging of everyday life, in one's regular environment, from next door, below, wherever.

Then, and this is what was thought after the experience had occurred more the once—a third knocking, which whether it is thought or not, when it is located leads to an instantaneous unity. All knocks are subsequently lost. The first time(s) this occurs, it is not understood, and perhaps forgotten about, not even realized.* However, searching oneself for a long time a second distinct occurrence jogs one's memory to a previous instance. One begins to think; the unity that results from locating the third knock turns everything inside out at once. One forgets what one ought really not to forget. The singularity of experience resulting, so suddenly, leaves no room for the plurality, which was so important just an instant previously.

The "volitional", as it is felt to be, it's plurality, and in each of the two of it's three aspects so briefly noticed, the lack of total personality; fragmentation; even, that it is non-personal: the three separated are incomplete, and yet together make up possibilities of activities of one's life, as though without the crisscrossing of those three lines one would not have being.

The self is schematized, in this paper, as consisting of interior and exterior, and it is thought that what happens is that the unity of the self-exterior has moved from without, inwards to the division between self-exterior and self-interior: reaching that division, the result is the effective loss of the exterior.

---

* One can hardly claim to have realized the third knock, let alone describe it.

As stated already, action is being considered as an inter-individual bond.

To return to what it was about action that seemed to require some emphasis, it seemed that what people do in their everyday lives is often careless; activities not fully intended or only fully realized after they have occurred, if they are not totally forgotten. The lack of total stillness, which is so common, leads one to wonder if there is a distinction to be drawn between actions, or levels of actions. Is the deed, which is deliberate, produced from full awareness, different somehow from what occurs involuntarily? There are uncertain reactive behaviors (scratching, twisting one's hair, wagging one's foot, all examples, though their mention may debase the argument, for one may add, it depends how one scratches or wags one's foot!)?

Only recently, the viewpoint here shifted. From a new position, joining determination with thought, it seems possible that the answer is not to dwell upon action in absolute or relative terms, but to dwell instead upon thought, in relation to actions.

Discussing the individual in relation to other individuals, the convention of referring to one side of the relation as the observer individual and the other side of the relation as alternative individual will be adapted. In fact, what is implied is that the observer individual is the subjective experiencer and thinker, the "you" or I, while alternative individual refers to any other person in relation to whoever is contemplating the relation.

Figure 2: Opposing individuals

Of course, the observer is an alternative individual to another or alternative individual. This leaves the distinctions as pointless, perhaps.

What is the difference between the action of an individual at one moment, and at another moment?

It is possibly unacceptable to imply that one person's thought has a bearing on another's activity. However, if one thinks about this, it is not so unreasonable; the fruits of peoples' thinking may have a very great deal to do with other's activities. Here, though, what was being implied was that a person's thought could affect another's activity, more or less as the thought occurred.

An acceptable way of stating this relation between thought and action is tentatively suggested as follows:—

Determinational thought, on the part of an individual observer, is that thought which occurs in correspondence with action on the part of an opposing individual.

Non-determinational thought, on the part of an individual observer, is that thought which accompanies the production of ambivalent form (this is not action) on the part of an individual alternative.

The understanding of determination and the terms usage have changed since the writer first dwelt it upon. Then, it was used along with the term experience. Since then, experience was reconsidered and it was decided that it was surely closely related to consciousness, more closely related than was being shown. The term experience was also obviously being used to refer to something, which it was eventually decided was order—something on a higher level than experience.

Now, thought is being termed as either determinational or non-determinational. Determinational thought is simply thought that is accompanied in a social context by action; i.e. determined thought in an observer individual arises corresponding with action in another or alternative individual who relates to the individual observer.

Non-determinational thought is that which arises in an individual observer without action relating the individual to other individuals. Instead, it is posited that this non-determinational thought arises corresponding with something other than action—something simpler—tentatively termed "ambivalent form" in or of another individual relating to the individual observer. The production and reception of this ambivalent form constitutes influence. Rather, when the ambivalent form is the interindividual bond, the state is known as influence.

So rather than look at the question as "what is the difference between action at one moment and another, in a specific individual?" one considers instead, and is stating the matter in the clearest way when postulating that "action on the part of the individual (individual alternative) who is in some direct relation to another individual (individual observer) implies determinational thought on the part of the latter individual (individual observer)".

Non-action, empty action, empty form or ambivalent form, all terms meaning the same thing here, is what occurs on the part of an individual alternative if an individual observer's thought is non-determination.

There has been a lot of uncertainty about this last term (ambivalent form). When a term was first sought for use here, ambivalent came to mind. Then, when connotations arising from psychoanalysis were thought of, "ambiguous" seemed possibly the more appropriate word to use. While well aware of what an ambiguous figure is from study of visual perception psychology, ambiguity was not what was meant to be implied. Instead, a valency of one or another was what was intended; with a change in direction of it's valency, but not of it's nature (see Figure 3).

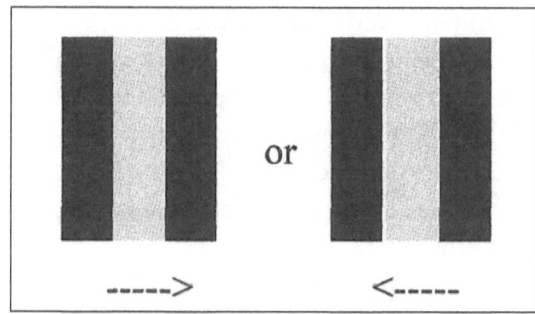

Figure 3. Ambivalent form—change in direction of valency

The ambivalent form is the opposite of consciousness. It is pregestural. This so called ambivalence lies in the fact that it is perceptible or not perceptible, depending on the condition of the observer.

General patterns of thought in opposing individuals are affirmable. (By this I mean they are saying yes.) Production of ambivalent form by an individual alternative serves as an undifferentiated basis for thought by an individual observer. In this sense, it is like a surface of constant agitation onto which the observer can map thought activity. If on this surface there is a saliency, this may be further characteristic of a pattern of thought. The one producing the undifferentiating ambivalent form amid which there is such a saliency may derive such a manner of form production from what they have learned of others' form production in relation to their own thought. There is the hope to facilitate the mode of thought in others that others, in them, have facilitated.

It is not implied that individuals can be conscious of the ambivalent form. Nor is it decided whether those who do not produce the ambivalent form so frequently as others are any more likely to be aware of the form. It is not a behavior easily accessible consciously.

Insofar as the ambivalent form production of the individual alternative necessitates thought or the mapping of thought to the ambivalent form, by the individual observer, then the observer will tend to avoid perception of what will not be in it's favor.

Perceived self-inadequacies may make it difficult to stand in the light of one's own consciousness. It is not stated that one can tell by looking at the schematization (Figure 4) whether anything is on or off. However, in social life, there is a leaning towards dependable ons and offs, which is a matter of consensus and learning.

Figure 4. Ambivalent form

When there is an influence on an individual, that person's thought retains a relative freedom lacking when the individual is exposed to action. Influences are not determined.

This is what was implied at the beginning, when it was suggested that there are those individuals in society who have for one reason or another a deficit in production of ambivalent form; and, that they may be penalized for their holistic insistence upon "action or nothing". Society has them as its focus. Those surrounding them are bound to think deterministically instead of being able to engage in whatever mental activity the members of society by default would drift towards. This is not bad for society, to have such focal points in its midst; but there is a penalty imposed on those who find themselves in this central position. Neither are the penalties all-bad. Something may be necessary to tame these individuals who find themselves, by virtue of their lack of form production, in positions of power, at the center of much that is going on around them in the world.

It is wished that emphasis be given to this point that influences are not determining, relatively speaking. The stimulus to think of influence came from the Raven—French type of analysis. The presentation here seems a novel way of considering what weight ought to be given influence.

One must give some weight to the other side of the matter: that action, true action, is of the highest achievements of the individual, and thus its occurrence in relation to opposing individuals ought to facilitate the most sublime of thinking on the part of those opposing individuals. Here, there may be a fine line between the determinational effect of another's action and one's own origination. Might there not be originations in tandem with others' action?

It began to seem that this work as a whole was becoming an exposition on thought. Several years ago, thought would not have been dwelt upon, it seeming altogether too complicated. It has been of first most importance to explain with the terms used here what projection is, and to decide for what it is actually responsible; for instance, what role is played in hallucinatory experience. An attempt was made to equate projection with the whole of what thought might be.

Projection, it was considered, involved sensory process and completion. It would not provide the motivation for thought. The ambivalent form derives from projection, as was shown in the example of Figure 1. Adding form to projection results in a break-up of projection into actional and ambivalent form.

This "form" that is added is what true form is for the experiencing, perceiving individual. The form comes from the individual, not from without.

The ambivalent form is also considered as a basic unit of sensory output; that is, a source of ambivalent form is sensing. The complete result of sensing is the projection structure, and as already indicated this structure naturally breaks down, producing the ambivalent form.

Joining the ambivalent forms into strings seems to be what happens while sensing, or is a natural consequence of the sensing. This may be confusing, but what is considered is that the ambivalent forms that are joined together are in part at least derived from other people—that is the ambivalent form that results from breakdown of the projection in one individual contributes to the formation of a projection in another individual.

Projection is only there for sensing, and sensing is only there to obtain ambivalent form for further projections. Breaking down the strings is associated with the projection, as if fulfillment of the projection.

If it is considered that perhaps not all sensing is projectional, a difficulty is encountered. It is similar to a difficulty that arises if one attempts to consider the relation between nourishment (or self-substantiation) and the origin of the individual—one cannot remove the social factor from nourishment.

JAMES P. DEVANEY

Similarly, the individual while exposed to an inanimate physical environment may be free from the ambivalent form of others, but could absorb or learn nothing new, only consolidate what they already have.

As mentioned later on in this work, it seems that the ambivalent form is to be characterized as a lack of stillness that nevertheless does not rank as movement. Therefore, a good way of describing it seems to be to refer to it as shifting.

It had been a worry, as the momentum of earlier times became less evident when approaching the system of description of mentality, centered on consciousness and using the primary-secondary schematics, that the work was not as compelling as would have been wished. If study of natural phenomenon, and in particular, disturbance, leads to understanding, forces can be harnessed. Without a problem one cannot hope to attain much.

Projectory phenomena of themselves do not pose significant problems for this writer. The question is, did they ever figure a problem at all? One is aware of very little in the way of teaching that was received on projection in the course of psychology classes. There is the T.A.T. and the Rorschach. Perhaps there is a little here that was yet pivotal.

It is felt that the phrase "sensory projection" indicates well that everything that is "out there" is put out there. This seems a strong sense of the term projection.

There is a story about an alcoholic who while suffering delirium tremens complained that there were elephants on the wall of the room in which he found himself. Then, there was a program on Irish television a couple of years ago that dealt with the life and work of the artist Louis le Brocquy. His technique, firing a splotch of paint onto the canvas, and then, with movements of the arm that seemed almost automatic or convulsive, working that blot of ink, carefully watching for the chance appearance of form that could be incorporated into a grander form. Whatever he would arrive at, it would not have the appearance of something that had been consciously wrought. This seems an instance when projection is captured. It is a bit like the elephants on the wall, except that in the artist's case, a peculiar condition is entered, and in an essential sense control is maintained. Relating the projection of the artist to that of the psychotic who hears voices, or places another, different construction on something that is spoken; it seems that in the latter case, control is lost or absent.

The strong sensory projection includes all perception of the environment—enclosures, furniture, etc. The projection of the artist and to some extent the psychotic would seem to be a weak form.

If the projection of the artist or disturbed individual remains ephemeral, it is because there is no idea formation component that can be developed. If the individual arrives at a point where the projection becomes concrete rather than ephemeral, as with phantom voices being heard, how can one attribute this to the development of idea formation?

Besides projection and idea formation there is action, which must be involved in the development of what is concrete in the environment. Perhaps by acting on the basis of what is only ephemeral, one way or another, in a manner that at first may be arbitrary, the ephemeral construct gains in strength, or rather the capacity to construct in such a manner becomes stronger.

It is as though a person lying watching the clouds decides that whichever item he imagines he sees first, a food-item or a drink-item, he will go and either eat or drink, depending on what was imagined to be seen; eventually, regardless of the specific content of the construction, the constructive (projectional) capability becomes stronger.

It might be considered that the understanding of projection is an insurmountable task. The hope here is that a coherent system of schematization, with sufficient inspiration of terminology, will indeed facilitate a description wherein the reactions of the organism are the disclosures of sensory mentality. The constructions, which are permitted and utilized at the same time as the disclosures, relate to meaning and derive from action, as projections.

The Primary and Secondary Principles in Relation to Self; Opposition; Union and Separation

(i)

THE PREDOMINATING VIEW here is that the primary and secondary principles are never absolutely separable in the human condition, and thus they have no absolute isolation unless it is as man represents them.

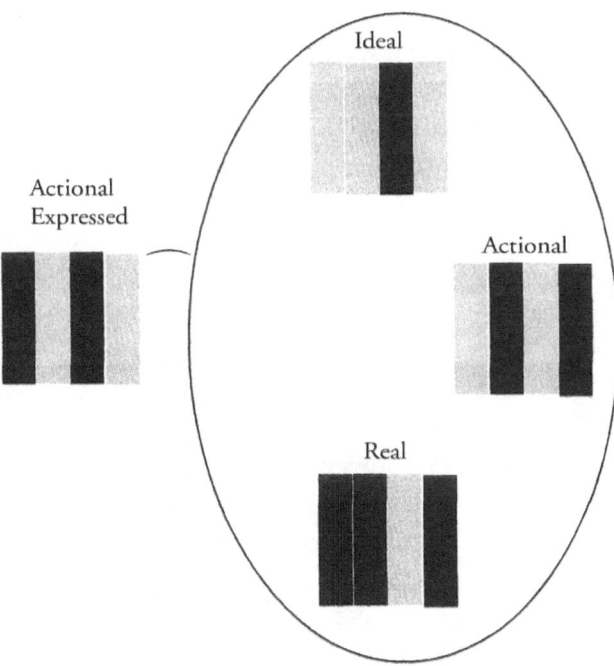

Figure 5. The Expression of the Actional

The description of the processed action, projection and idea formation intra-individually, refers to the origin of these processes, and they are subsequently termed originating processes. Yet, action is also considered as evident interindividually, as when it arises as a bond between individuals. This must depend on the expression of the actional by individuals (Figure 5).

The opposing view, of principles that never lose their nature, nor are altered or mixed, though they are represented together, permits one to take a useful view of separation and the social condition.

With interindividual relations (of separation) origins are not evident, as they are in the intra-individual condition of union.

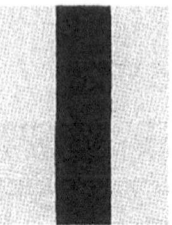

Figure 6. Consciousness

To make clear what this inseparability vs. separability of the principles means, and why it is brought up; the primary and secondary principles are considered in (both) heterogeneous combinations, that is primary and secondary mixed together, as in the schema of consciousness (two primaries with a secondary in between—see Figure 6); and, homogeneously, for example as all three or four primaries together, as in restriction or power.

The difference between the primary and secondary principles shows, with a homogeneous combination, if separability is allowed, but only in relation to heterogeneous combinations with separability not allowed.

The primary principle in isolation is considered complete. That is, a single instance of the primary has a sufficiency.

The secondary principle, however, in isolation, or, a single instance of the secondary, is characterized as incomplete. It is necessary that the secondary be represented plurally before one refers to it as having completion (see Figure 7).

So with consciousness represented as a single secondary between two primary elements, incompletion of the secondary principle is evident.

Evidence of the secondary nature in this manner is like a pinpointing of materiality, and this is another way of thinking of consciousness.

The secondary principle is equated with materiality, while the primary principle is equated with temporality.

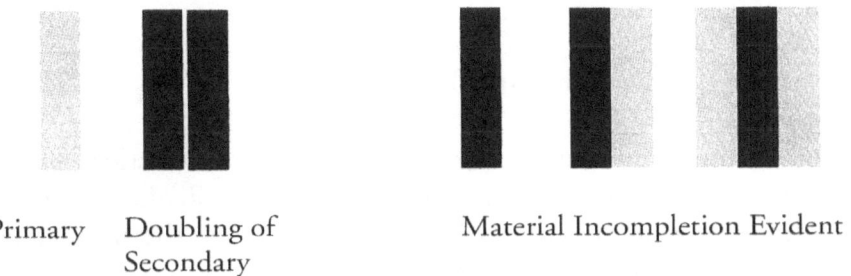

Primary   Doubling of   Material Incompletion Evident
          Secondary

Figure 7. Completion vs. Material Incompletion

Another way of stating it is that consciousness depends on the nature of the material.*

The inseparability and separability of the principles as mentioned above are used to describe union and separation of the self.

If it is acceptable that separation of the principles always implies that the secondary is part of a plurality, or represented as such, then at separation both the primary and secondary are complete, and they are indistinguishable from each other on grounds of incompletion of the one principle.

With inseparability of the principles, however, it is implied that consciousness will make evident the incomplete nature of the material or secondary.

The distinction between the two cases then, is that while materiality is distinguishable with inseparability of the opposing principles, it requires a comparison of the two states, separability vs. inseparability, to make evident that there is a temporality.

Since temporality is indistinguishable from materiality (on the basis of completion) with separability of the principles (the secondary always plural), it takes the contrasting situation of inseparability of principles before there is a possibility of the temporality being disclosed.

---

* Here, The I Ching is quoted: Hexagram 2, Line 2 (p.390—part of the extended commentaries) "for in the nature of the earth lies the light." (This is attributed to the Confucian School—see Introduction to the Material, Book II, pp.257-58, note five). I Ching, The Chinese Book of Changes, Wilhelm/ Baynes version, The Bollingin Series, Princeton University Press.

To use an analogy: it is like inseparability means "black", while separability means "grey"—the light (or temporal) is only evident as a contrast on the part of the grey, or separable condition, in relation to the black of inseparability. Here, blackness is material (due to consciousness), but there is no lightness evident or temporality per se.

(ii) Opposition

An inconceivable opposition between the self-exterior and the self-interior is now being considered, and certain "reconciliation with reason" of the inconceivable opposition is possible by linking the inconceivable aspect to the abysmal or unbridgeable nature of time: time considered as discrete and of the self-exterior.

Is it possible that there is a sense in which the different conditions of self, union and separation, are not comparable at all, and that is in the temporal-sequential sense?

If time is at the division between self-exterior and self-interior (having "moved inward" by contraction of the exterior or expansion of the interior), the condition of the self is termed separate, and that is what is meant by separation. In this condition, there is effectively no division between exterior and interior, or rather the exterior / interior dichotomy vanishes. Subsequently, all consideration of interaction of the self is in social terms, in relation to other individuals. Prior to this, one considers the self in its own terms, as exterior to interior, or, in terms of interior processes.

Besides this self-exterior / self-interior dichotomy, there is another pairing of sides—that of the two halves of the self-interior itself. With a duality of the interior, an opposition of one side of the interior and the other side of the interior is termed conceivable.

An absolute separation (unbridgeable) at the division between exterior and interior is considered to be the condition when the self is separate; but also as the interior duality has approached bearing a conceivable opposition.

An absolute separation (unbridgeable) outside of the division between exterior and interior is considered as the exterior has an inconceivably opposite content with regard to the interior. The inconceivability is attributed or linked to time; the condition described is the prerequisite for union.

The idea used above is that, if there is an absolute separation at the division between exterior and interior, there is in effect no division. Rather, there is only an interior, and that loses the distinction as an interior (which

JAMES P. DEVANEY

was possible when the exterior was present or within reach). And with neither an exterior or an interior the only interaction the self is capable of is social, between selves.

With union, origins are described intra-individually. Three originating processes are ascribed to the interior: projection, idea formation and action. The only separation that action may have from the self is within the self, although it is considered as a bond interindividually.

(iii)

Idea formation, as an attempt to conceive with regard to the content of the self-exterior: when the absolute separation lies outside of the division between exterior and interior in the exterior, brings to prominence bridging for what it is.

Idea formation is thought of as a uniting process; idea is formed, but is never present to the opposite, because separation occurs, and idea is thus only for socially based considerations available.

One has just stated it is impossible to pin union down—as soon as there is union, separation occurs to keep idea from its "inconceivable opposite".

Absolute separation "withdrawing" to the division between exterior and interior results in a conceivable opposition being produced on the interior; that is, opposites are produced for the duality of the interior.

One wishes to claim that the resulting pair of opposites now available on the self-interior bear direct relation to each other as the inconceivable-opposition pair, of exterior and interior, would relate to each other if such a relation was possible. In fact, this latter relation is by definition impossible. Also, it is just at this point, with a dual pair on the interior, that no division between exterior and interior can be found (in fact, the inner duality must be relinquished too).

As the exterior / interior dichotomy disappears, so too the duality, present in the interior, is lost. Instead, there is a threefold unity, the unity in the actional of two opposing side. This is a social unity.

Some time back it was put forward that the actional is expressed whenever there is a "contraction" of the self (see Figure 5 again).

(iv)

Idea formation is like an unfolding in the developing individual. A complete determinism does not occur, and it is suggested that this is because it is ultimately an endless process. The individual's idea formation does not wind on and on deterministically, but is countered. In the secondary principle, or rather a particular grouping of it, one finds a unitary nature that differs from that of the primary. This unitary nature can oppose the primary unity (see Figure 8) and in doing so is termed boundary.

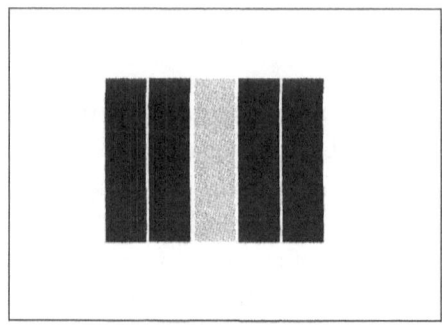

Figure 8. Boundary

When one considers what is termed the inconceivable opposition between the self-exterior and the self-interior at union, and that one has proposed that there is a sense in which one cannot know of the ultimate nature of that content of the exterior (termed inconceivably opposite), one looks to ideal, deriving from the self-interior and finds that it is not in any relation of opposition to that content of the exterior termed inconceivable, but in relation to the real, which derives from boundary of the interior. Boundary is the opposite of idea formation.

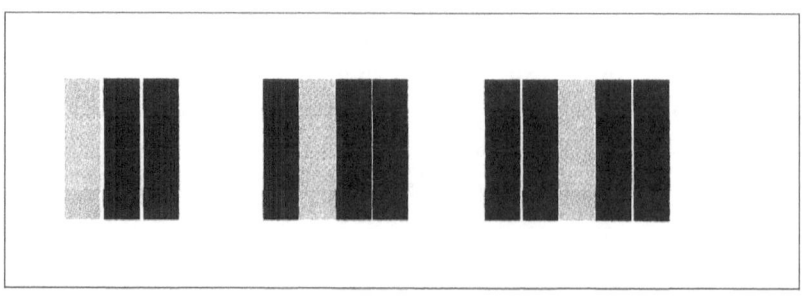

Figure 9. Movement, Real and Boundary

Boundary depicts equilibrium of the two sides around the primary.

Movement is the absence of that equilibrium; on one side of the primary, no secondary (see Figure 9, first of three diagrams).

Real is depicted as one secondary on one side of the primary, and a pair of secondaries on the other.

At this point, it is interesting to consider that what was termed the ambivalent form has material sufficiency only as one secondary must depend for material completion on the other across the intervening primary. With real, one side of the primary has material completion without regard for the other side, though that other side may gain completion by reference to a secondary of the complete side (see Figure 10).

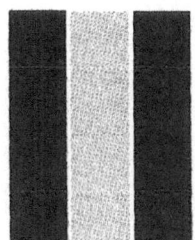 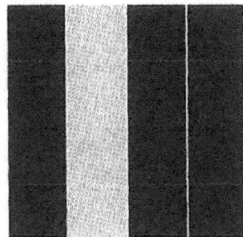

Figure 10. Ambivalent Form vs. Real

The schematics, by the use of single or paired elements, represent dynamisms in what is hopefully a very simple manner; one opposed to two, across an element, for instance, the resulting dynamism is characterized by the separating element: and the nature of the elements paired or separate.

(v)

With the opposition of the primary order and secondary order (order as it is termed here meant is the sense of command) one does point to what has been called the inconceivable opposition of the self-exterior and self-interior (see Figure 11).

This may help to understand what is meant by order in this discussion, though it does not help much explaining what has been termed inconceivably opposite content of the self-exterior. However, since the exterior / interior dichotomy disappears, one is left considering not the self-exterior, but the individual in relation to others and what arises between individuals.

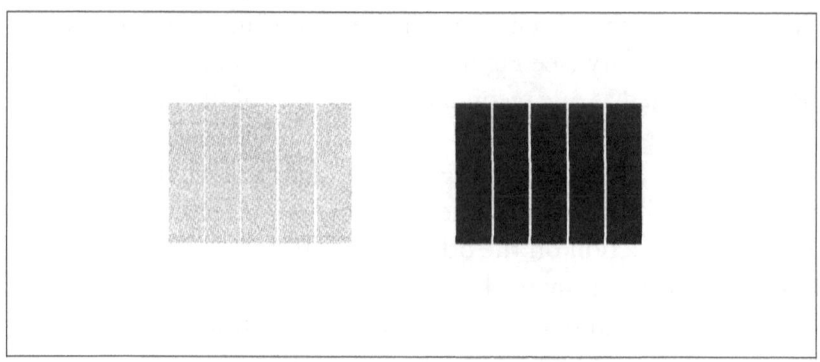

Figure 11. The Primary and Secondary Order

SECTION II

The Four Primary Combinations

(i) Idea

THE PRIMARY ELEMENT, modeled upon the yang principle of The Chinese Book of Changes; and with its opposite the yin principle, both claimed as integral to the Taoist system, though there is also the view that the I Ching and its use of the two principles predates Taoism (and was probably important in the formation of Taoism); here, in a thoroughly speculative manner, is linked to the psychological principles as these are formulated.

It is easier to deal with only one half of the opposition, in this case, the yang or light principle, denoting masculinity and firmness. The yin or dark principle, symbolizes femininity and yieldingness, is not ignored; however, it is true to say that one has not led with this yin or secondary principle, but has waited and tried to relate it in an overall picture by mirroring; trying to find how it might fit if there actually was a mirroring.

When it was considered at first that the primary might relate well to what psychologists know of as inhibition or as an "inhibitory principle", no thought was immediately given to what this would mean when a secondary principle or its psychological manifestation was sought. An assumption that the primary implied temporality and the secondary implied materiality seemed sufficient.

The fault with equating the primary with temporality seemed to be that temporality was not a strong enough or high enough term. From The Book of Changes, the primary is Heaven, or the heavenly, and time results from the movement of this Heaven.

Assuming a relation between the primary and inhibition derives simply from the observation that psychological processes require time, and many fundamental psychological processes are inhibitory in nature.

When it was seriously considered what the secondary stood for in psychological terms, what came to mind was an associating of a doubling of the secondary with something like realm, with which one was not completely comfortable. What was meant was that a doubling of the secondary would be an opposite of idea, placedness without a place. The secondary could not be defined, in isolation or singularity, as the primary was.

The inability of the secondary to stand on its own came to be seen as a characteristic of the secondary, as discussed in Section I above. This in turn frees one from having to have an exact mirroring of function for the secondary combinations (see Figure 12).

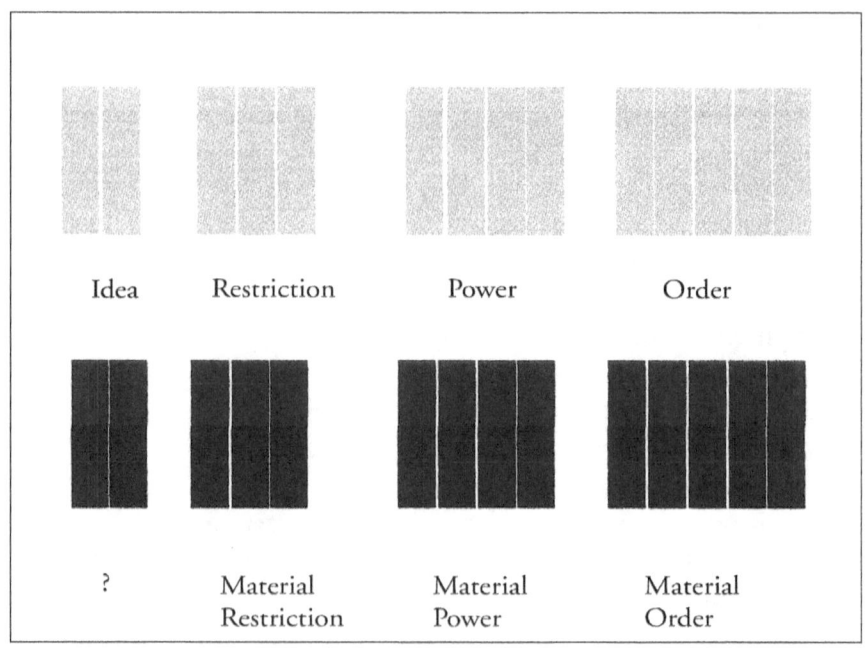

Figure 12. The Primary vs. Secondary Combinations

The secondary combinations corresponding to the primary "restriction", "power" and "order" may best be labeled "material–restriction", "material-power" and "material-order", but no compulsion is there to so label the secondary correspondent to idea (and "material idea" does not seem such a useful term anyway).

Again, the rational for this discrimination with regard to the secondary correspondent to idea is that, with a single instance of the secondary, there is incompleteness. A plurality of the secondary is required before completion is evident, and with a doubling of the secondary, completion is just evident, giving this combination some of the character of the single primary.

Idea as a doubling of the primary or inhibitory principle is considered as disinhibitory. It is thought of as that which is related to what may evoke in the absence of a stimulus. In motional aftereffects, although there is a physiological explanation, the aftereffect and its diminishment with time can be seen as a stimulus effect and it's countering.

One is not implying causal principles here; but what countering there may be of such an effect may relate to what may stand for the stimulus in its absence.

Since there are all kinds of aftereffects, it is not the physiological basis that is important in this context, but the fact that a countering is evinced.

(ii) Restriction

Restriction is a completely new term thought of while devising the primary schemata. That it has lasted may be due to subjective factors on the part of the writer. With this new term, much of the discussion on power and order was able to develop.

At first, restriction was thought of as the result of a reduction on a set of ideas. Restriction in its conventional usage denotes a "thou shalt not" or a prohibition of action. Just as idea as it is discussed here is a sort of positive thing, consisting of a pairing or pitting against each other of two inhibitory or negative elements (like—1 x—1), so restriction is seen as a negative thing; it is idea with a further application of the inhibitory or negative principle (like—1 x—1 x—1). Restriction as arising from a set of ideas and at the same time negative implies the focusing on something that is not idea itself.

Restriction is itself not idea. This is where restriction in association with idea, as order, comes into play. Order, as discussed later, considered as idea "with" restriction, is the idea "of" restriction. This means order is an identity.

But, it may be added; idea is itself something of an identity. Here, the view is taken that this identity of idea is weak. It is with restriction, where one has a set of ideas reduced that stronger identity appears. Yet, restriction is not idea. The association of idea with restriction is order, and is strong identity.

With order one has a changing point from the negatives of the primary and restriction to the positives of idea and power.

While considering aftereffect to see if idea could be derived or isolated, it seemed that idea could not be separated from any aspect of the perceptual problem. It seems, quite simply, that idea is not separable from form. Although one can represent idea by a doubling of the primary, and form as a pairing of a single primary with a single secondary, this does not imply that, given the general correctness of the procedure, idea should be distinguishable from form.

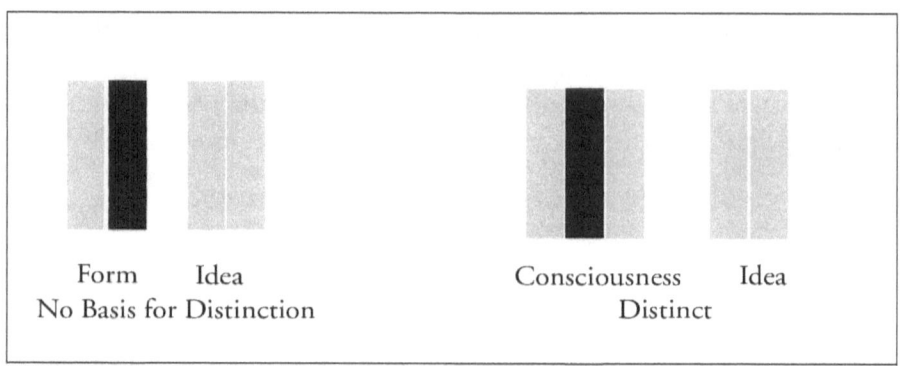

Figure 13. Idea and Form

With consciousness, there is a sandwiching of the secondary between two primaries, and one says of this arrangement that the secondaries nature is emphasized or pinpointed. Likewise with the ambivalent form, the secondary gains completion because it is present in plurality, although it must reach across an intervening primary to achieve that (Figures 3 & 4).

With a single instance of the primary together with a single instance of the secondary (see Figure 13), the primary can get no directionality from the secondary on account of its incompleteness (unlike with the ambivalent form where there is directionality, though it is ambivalent or shifting one way or another) (see Figure 3 again).

Since restriction is more complex than idea there was a hope that separation from form would not be such an insoluble problem.

There is also a moral aspect to the usage of the term restriction. While this was not at once seen to be good, psychologically speaking, eventually the opinion that if there was a moral side to restriction, there could also be a non-moral side to it too. The non-moral side is what would be sought and used in this discussion, while recognizing that a moral aspect was not only unavoidable, but also realistic, when approaching problems from which one did not wish to derive a never ending sequence of further problems.

Form, described as a single primary with a single secondary, also implies being, as the principles represent what is primordial. They may also imply space, as the condition of being, a condition with two limits (only one of which is complete).

This treatment of form as being certainly implies causality, whereas causality was eschewed when regarding idea as a concomitant of aftereffect. Perhaps one must have a pairing of opposites before cause can be considered.

(iii) Power

The impetus to discuss power in the same terms of consciousness employed everywhere in this paper must have been underlying even the first efforts to devise descriptive schemata. Power is here considered as related to influence as it is in the article on "The Social Bases of Power" which is indicative of the approach of authors Raven and French. When this article was first read, it was found to be very stimulating. However, there were a couple of points about their approach that right away did not seem completely correct.

The Raven and French discussion on power and influence was very methodical and attempted to describe the dynamics of influence in mechanistic terms. After reading their presentation one cannot help feeling that in actuality most if not all social interactions concerning influence are unconscious. Their mechanistic approach implies that the relevant factors of influence can and ought to be measurable (perhaps by some sort of a sociometric method, or by inventing a closed system wherein all reward is identifiable or measurable). Perhaps preconscious is a better term to use, but certainly what is involved in influence need in no way be conscious as it occurs. Subsequent to influence, the individual might attempt to bring into the light of consciousness relevant factors, but this is by no means inevitable, and might be a basis for what one decides is relatively intelligent behavior (the reflection on what influences may have pertained in a given situation).

Power as an aspect of the relations between target and source in the influence-situation is, besides unconsciousness, another problem difficult to understand on the basis of what was in the Raven-French article.

Power must be considered as lying on both sides of the relation between individuals. Though this is described further as this paper develops, it is mentioned here that the distinction between what lies on one side of the relationship, and, what lies on both sides of the relationship, is made, and considered as follows: the absolute separation which it is proposed lies as an abyss between all beings, makes it impossible for there to be any cognizance on the part of the one individual as to what that most intimate condition of the other actually is; while, at the same time a new view as to the nature of order, and a classification of order as either light or dark (primary or secondary) does permit one to consider the being has access to an "all" of inter-relatedness, which all sensory constructs and projections tend to faithfully reconstruct (in the natural course of things), so while the target is protected as it were from the source, it is not deprived of what via the primary order is an access to, in perfection, what actually pertains.

Consider how influence is described in Figure 14. This is meant to show what lies on the part of the observer. Power is separated on the observer's side of the interindividual bond by the ambivalent form (influence).

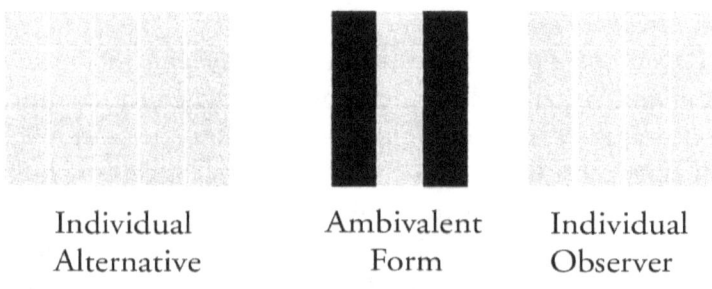

| Individual | Ambivalent | Individual |
| Alternative | Form | Observer |

Figure 14. The Observer's Construct

The order on the left is meant to represent the order of the individual opposing individual observer, while power on the right is meant to show the power of the observer himself. It all lies on the part of the observer, though. The order on the left is the observer's construction of what there may be on the part of individual alternative.

Again, consider the position when action is the inter-individual bond instead of influence. The schema is of what the observer constructs lies on the other side of the relation, as well as his own (Figure 15).

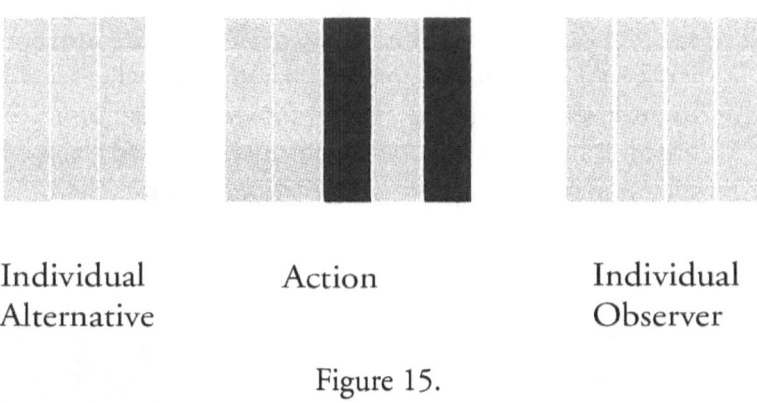

Individual
Alternative

Action

Individual
Observer

Figure 15.

(iv) Order

Below are some schemata, all intended to show what lies on the side of a single individual.

Basal

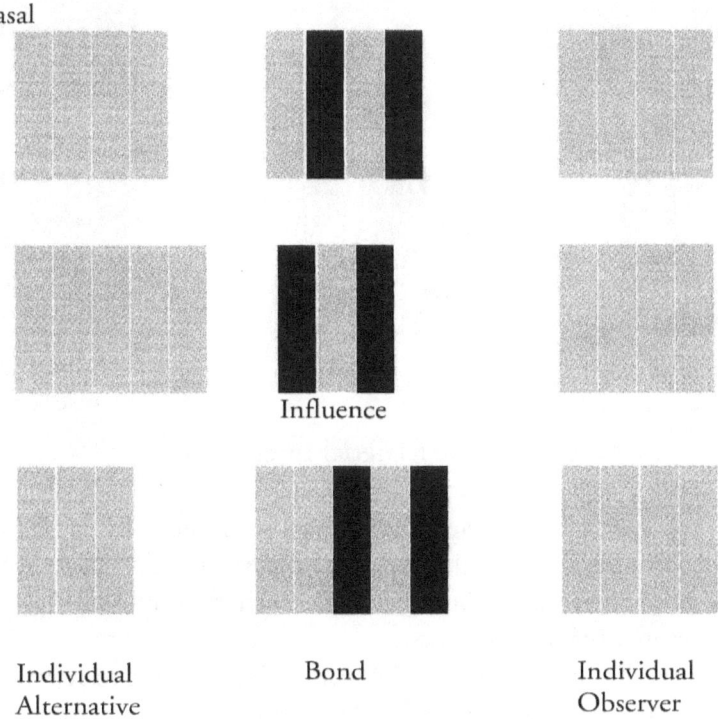

Influence

Individual
Alternative

Bond

Individual
Observer

Figure 16a. Non-material Interrelations

On the left in Figure 16 are constructions intended to represent what must lie on the part of another or an alternative individual. Of course, the observer individual can have no direct knowledge of that construction, or what it is that the construction represents, based upon what the observer can derive from the situation at the given moment. Instead, one goes back to infantile learning and what has developed since then and claims that the observer is able to hypothesize with great assurance what is there.

Basal

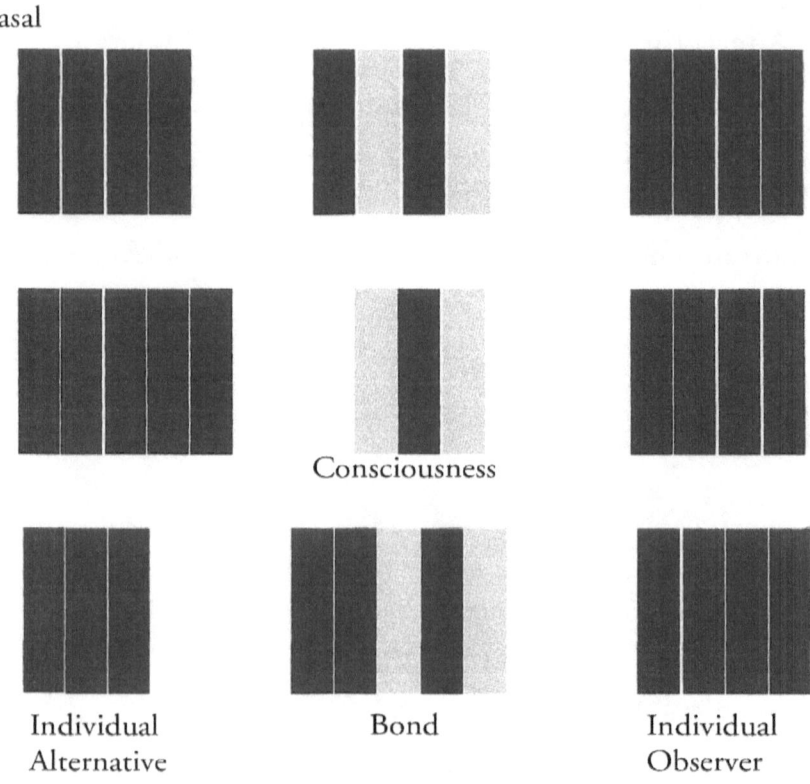

Consciousness

Individual   Bond   Individual
Alternative   Observer

Figure 16b. Material Interrelations

One has just stated that there must be some sort of an absolute separation, an abyss, at the limits of the observer individual, over which one does not receive any contact from another individual, nor perhaps from inanimate objects either.

In the middle in the figure are constructions meant to represent what interindividual bond there might be. The basal position is with the actional in the middle, as an interindividual bond. Here, the alternative individual's exterior is hypothesized as having the same elemental configuration as individual observer, that is, with four primary (or secondary) elements.

As can be seen, action as an interindividual bond arises when, as depicted, the four elements on the left (of individual alternative) goes to three, or power goes to restriction. Power is still remaining on the right side (here that is individual observer). So, a basic interrelation with action as interindividual bond implies that there is power on the one hand and restriction on the other.

Also interesting is the situation when the ambivalent form is the interindividual bond. Here, power is on the one hand, and order on the other. A major postulate has arisen of always attributing order to the individual alternative. Thus, as described a bit further later, power is always prioritized or available to individual observer before order.

Also, order takes on a role of identity, and thus identity is never with the observer, though the observer may support a great number of alternative identities.

Much of what has developed here regarding power and order was in an attempt to justify the following statement: "Power must be prioritized with regard to order." What is implied is that there is a tendency in mental activity to "run aground" or enter a stasis. This is attributed to when order comes to dominate a process of thought. The strong way to proceed is from idea, via restriction to power, and then order is a culmination. The fault that is found is that the order occupies a place in the scheme, and it is as though order bears backwards on power; order contains the completeness of will, and it is a cogent presence, even though the necessary steps to arrive at order have not been thoroughly performed. An excellent example of this phenomenon is seen in the case of a small child who insists that he or she "knows", but who when pressed to express finds themselves at a loss. It is the view taken here that not just in childhood is this a problem but in more mature life also. The order is a handicap if its presence deters the work necessary to justify the order. This work is called prioritizing power with regard to order.

Order is viewed as "restriction associated idea". With power, however, a breaking down of the four primaries into smaller groups as done with order is not as easy.

It is suggested that to consider power as an association of idea with idea, or of restriction with a single primary, is not very helpful on its own.

It is thought instead that order and power have at one point equivalence. That is, at some point, order, considered as restriction in association with idea, is equivalent with power, and when this equivalence is present, power is to be considered as a fluctuating state (see Figure 17).

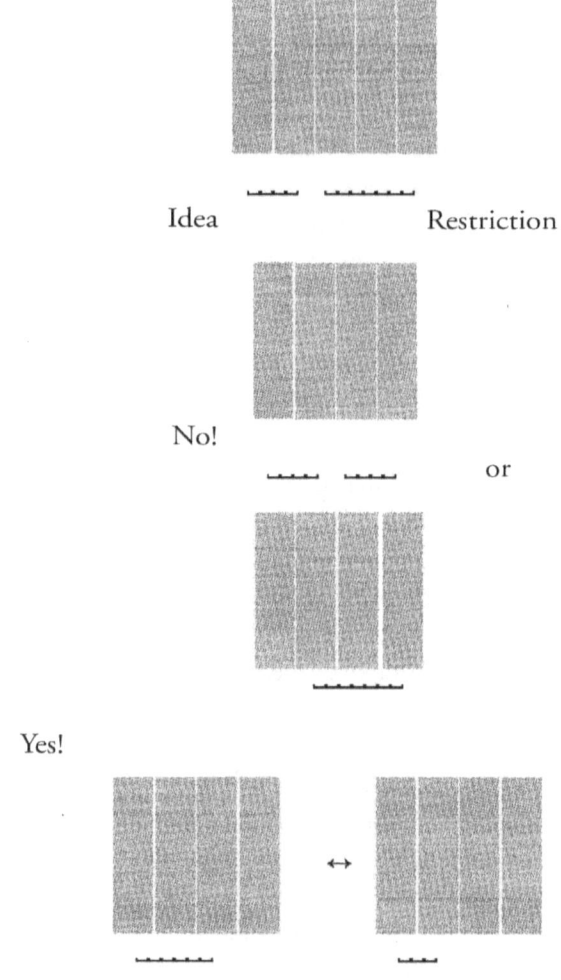

Figure 17.

In this case, power is able to demonstrate the same association of restriction with idea that order itself does. To effect this association, power fluctuates between conditions wherein restriction is distinct and a condition in which idea is distinct. The back-and-forth between these two conditions provides the association of restriction with idea that gives power equivalence with order.

JAMES P. DEVANEY

Power is never superior to order.

Order is always viewed, during influence, as lying on the part of the individual opposed to the individual with power, and is never considered as lying on the part of the observer. That is, the observer is the one with power; the opposing individual has order. In this manner, power is prioritized—order is always on the part of the other.

Admittedly, this is a novel approach, and it is perhaps a device necessary to the work of the subject matter of this paper, as much as it reflects true conditions in interindividual relations. To this prioritization is attributed the motivational foundation of thought, or the dynamic of thought. It is like the progression from the fourth to the fifth, or from power to order.

Another novel concept that is mentioned as having relevance to the discussion on thought is that there must be a correct restriction in order for union to occur. Recall that the exact point of union was hard to pin down—one could describe events up to the point before union, and then not again until the separation immediately contingent upon uniting. This implies that morality as well as temporality is related psychologically to action and thought. Whatever else morality may imply, it is meant to convey the notion of social consensus. Temporality, although it may not be thought of often in this fashion, is closely related to reward or what is of positive value. For instance, if an organism is in a state of distress, its temporal sense becomes of acute importance—if suffering is over with seemingly quickly, it is preferable to the interminable sense of events.

Assigning value to action is one of the notions found in the I Ching. In the fifty-fourth hexagram, titled "The Marrying Maiden", there is reference in the discussion on the fifth line to value of action. Perhaps not in every sense, but certainly in a mundane sense, this line refers to one of the ultimate conditions of experience. This hexagram was for the writer one of the most profound of all in The Book of Changes. The oriental philosophy stated explicitly in the Commentary on the Decision is that, if heaven and earth do not unite, all creatures fail to prosper. The judgment contained in this hexagram superficially seems to indicate very bad auspices: one should not seek to go anywhere or do anything. It is not to reinterpret the old saying, but to give an insight into the thought that at times while dealing with this book must border on the delusional, and perhaps does become deluded at times, that it is added now: that ill-boding judgment can help the reader who is possibly in an altered state of consciousness while using the book anyway (this from the meditational nature of the approach one develops towards the book) by helping one to the realization that at that instant and in that condition described by the structures of the hexagram, if the observer would only desist completely from all purposeful activity, it would be possible to attain to or maintain that which is most desirable in terms of attitude or regard for one's self condition.*

Power has no value assigned to it, as action may have.

When action has a positive value for the observer, what more can be desired (this is an interpretation of the oriental philosophy, with which the writer agrees)? Negative value of action, if such is possible, and if it is persisted with, seems a situation similar to what the Indians term Karma—an inability to break with an inferior behavior; doomed to live that way until somehow the organism learns to escape from it's negative action. It seems important to distinguish between power and the action-with-value that is so desirable and which depends upon power (see Figure 15).

---

* It is not known whether the "Bollingen Series XIX" copy of the Wilhelm / Baynes translation the writer is using in the U.S.A. has the exact same page numbering as the book available in Europe (the text seems identical). If this is the case, see pp. 664-668.

JAMES P. DEVANEY

SECTION III

Interindividual Relations and Thought

(i) The Primary Order and Projection as a Construction

O NE HAS A base understanding of order in the description "restriction associated idea"; here, order is broken up into a triplet and a pair with association the manner of joining. That this is a base manner of description is because there are no equivalent terms with which to describe order—only inferior combinations—restriction and idea. It may be of some help to keep in mind this base description of order; it is as an insider's view.

Another view of order, an outside view which has no immediately evident reconciliation with the inside view, and which is not a base description, arises from the past consideration of the creativity of the self which expresses the actional. Creativity is meant as an instance of the origin assigning itself as separate from itself the origin.

Figure 18.

Self Exterior

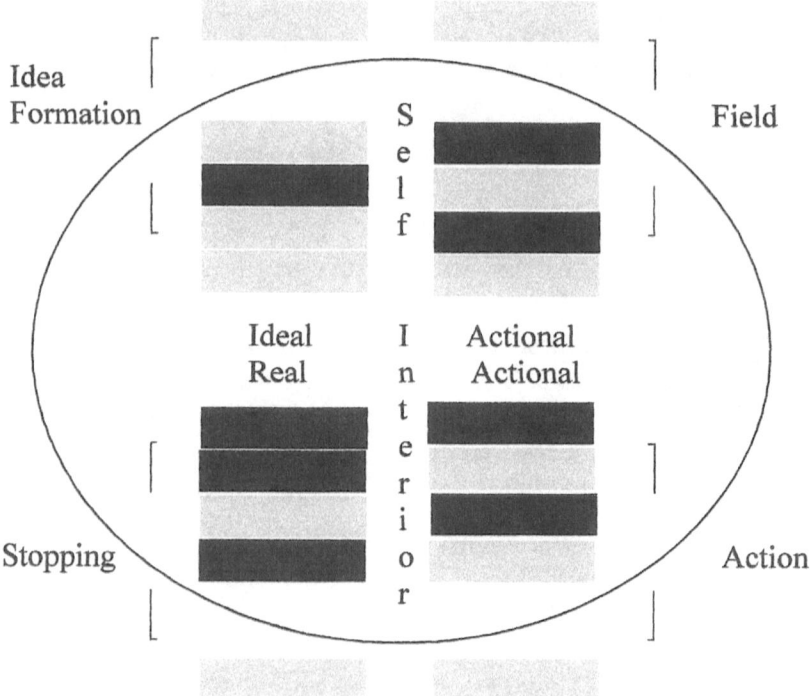

It happens when at unity of self, the interior, resolving originating processes (idea formation, action and field) prior to separation, diminishes each process from five-fold to four-fold (see Figure 18). Then, Ideal-Real-Actional-Actional goes to Ideal-Real-Actional as the other actional gains exteriorization (see Figure 5).

It is attributed to this originality or creativity of self, that expression of the actional occurs. Actional may be a fundamental of meaning.

However, the creativity of this occurrence necessitates a denial or negating. It is a negating of what has occurred. The negating is necessary to isolate as perfectly separate what formerly belonged to the interior. A better term than negating in this context is forgetting. Insofar as this general scheme is acceptable, it is also postulated that a continuous "forgetting" is an attribute of this fundamental process: resolving originations at union or between union and separation. It is implied that this forgetting, an instantaneity, is yet a continuity, constantly necessary to erase the link between what is expressed and the self-interior.

At that point, having decided on denial as an attribute of the process; and stepping back, so to speak, from the whole scheme of self (self in isolation [union]—self in relation [separation]; this seems a paradoxical manner of expressing it): one wishes to use the combination of pure or separate principles, homogeneous arrangements of primary on the one hand, secondary on the other, vs. a heterogeneous combination of both principles together to help illustrate separateness vs. union. It became apparent there was an aspect of the description, a presumption, which was not being taken into account*. One then fitted the denial or forgetting to the presumption involved; and while this is a bit fortuitous, to use a salient end of reflections to underpin the beginning of all the descriptions, it merges and gives a far-reaching background to what was felt to be the most valuable of all the processes to be explained, if possible: projection.

To describe this merging specifically: the primary order, as opposed to the secondary order, began to be used in a superior, non-base manner of description. By the primary order is now meant a "light social universe", as opposed to the dark social universe or secondary order.

An analogy is made with the physical universe as known. This may be understood as, on one level at least, an infinite void wherein lie points of light—points which themselves are vast—yet in relation to the immense spaces separating them are but points.

It is not intended that the analogy be pushed far.

The above universe of physics corresponds with a "dark universe"; one where there is a void containing sources. Using the term void is difficult, since if one carries it so far as to imply "void of space" one has nothing to go on in analogy.

However, one keeps it simple by raising the other part of the analogy, the light universe. Here, no void, but an intricacy of interrelation of or among, not point sources, but, as near as one can describe, point absences. The "point absence" is somehow easier to mention than void. There point

---

* This presumption is very difficult to express. In figures 14 or 15 for instance, one attempts to indicate what belongs to the other individual's exterior (the leftmost order or restriction, respectively), when in fact one bases an argument on an absolute separation, the other side of which one cannot pretend to be able to make the semblance.

absences (points of being they are likened to) are continuous forgetters, denying the vast interrelatedness to which they are constantly exposed.

So to end the analogy, there is the social world, among beings, where they can be viewed as points of light in a void where relations are to be worked out in terms of their own beings. This is the dark social universe or secondary order.

The light social world or primary order is when the being is emphasized rather as an absence, constant forgetter in a strict sense, continuously exposed to an "all" of interrelations; where the all is first and foremost always singularly and primarily evident—and necessarily, instantaneously and immediately, perpetually, forgotten.

Then, projection: what one is called upon every instant to restart afresh—a construction of what is already in infinite perfection manifest to the being.

The self will then have its constructions to retain, however imperfect.

(ii) Action, Idea and Intent

From without, action on the part of an individual alternative has to find correspondence with action of the infant observer individual. What arises on the infant-observer's part is an action that is in inverse relation to the action of individual alternative (see Figure 19).

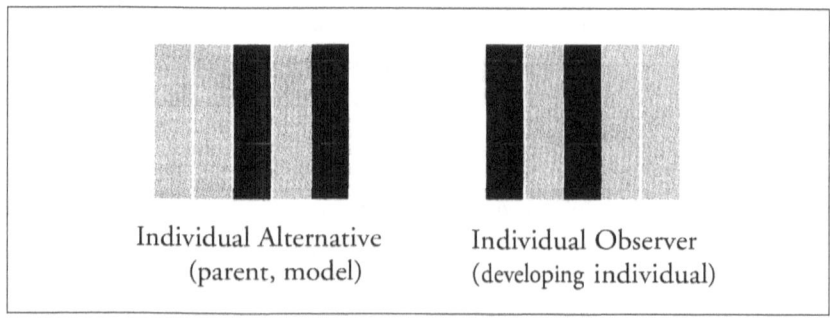

Individual Alternative
(parent, model)

Individual Observer
(developing individual)

Figure 19.

In addition to the inversion, there is a size or immediacy–following–sensation factor; the form of another is perceived as more distant, diminished than form sensed by inter-receptors of the individual's own body.

JAMES P. DEVANEY

Idea as a part of action is part of the origination of the action. One refers to this idea that is a component of the parent or model individual's action as intent. This is intent as an aspect of action.

The developing individual also has idea as a component of action originating. Again, action is considered strictly as an origination, not a reaction.

The task for nature in the development of the individual's relations to others, seems to be to allow the individual to base their actions' interpretiveness, or intent of action, on a gentle meeting between the two—developing and developed. Perhaps by imitation, common play-like activity of youth, this is possible.

In the course of play activity the developing observer individual does something exactly similar to another individual. Then, he or she is able to take cognizance of what idea or intent they share in that incidence of mutual, similar activity. The person relates the observable forms of individual alternative (derived from sensation), as by inversion to his own form production for those incidents.

How does the child "know" the other has performed similarly? This co-origination is viewed as a process that takes up the two individuals involved.

The inversional matching pivots on intent. That these nascent activities necessarily involve inchoate intent (relatively non-differentiated) in no way precludes a more differentiated origination of intent in relation to sharable forms as development progresses.

The intent of individual alternative may in later development be matched in and by individual observer on the basis of the ambivalent form derived from action of individual alternative (what is available here to individual observer is sensory information, basically the ambivalent form of action).

What may be traumatic in early life is when the developing individual meets with others who produce the form without the intent. Only in the long run can the individual observer be relatively sure of the correctness of the intent assigned.

If the individual observer assigns intent and it is in agreement, refer to this as the action on the part of individual alternative having content.

If the individual observer assigns intent and there is for some reason no match with individual alternative, in the long run this becomes evident.

Actions interpretivity will diminish or consequences will be lacking.

(iii)Ambivalent Form, Influence and Field

The individual, by being, produces form (form considered as a single primary joined to a single secondary). It is proposed that it is the being's prerogative to affect everything within itself with this form, continuously.

As in Figure 1, this form affects projection, a sensory process involving completion, and there is a breakdown of projection resulting in the ambivalent form and actional.

The individual's senses acquire ambivalent form, and with the ambivalent form derived from this breakdown of projection, further projection occurs.

That is, the projection consists of ambivalent form chains and the ambivalent form derives from individual observer and individual alternative.

If an individual alternative produces ambivalent form without intent, an unusual thing to occur it might seem at first, the individual observer has to decide that it is without intent. A further thing for individual observer would be to cope with a flood of such empty forms. With action, error assigning intent leads to consequences that are discordant. With ambivalent form, field is what provides a gauge as to whether an end of a sequence of ambivalent form is in accord with what society permits. Society determines what ambivalent form production is acceptable. That is, society determines what influences are permissible.

Figure 20.

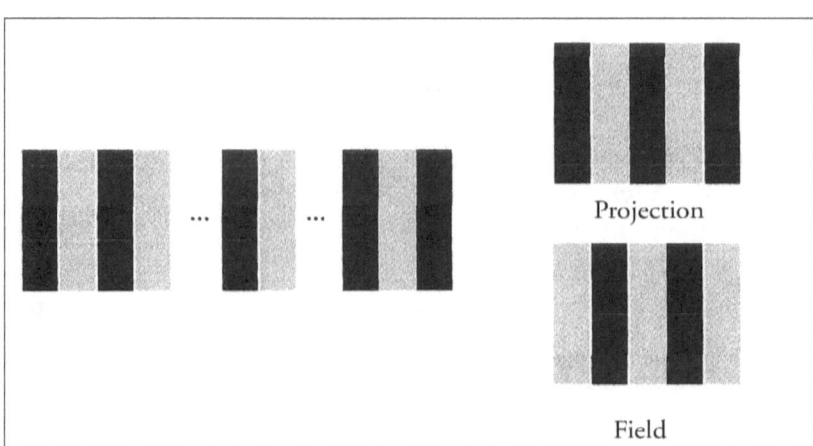

If the ambivalent form can be produced continuously and joined, giving a pattern at its simplest projection (see Figure 20), the opposite, field, has to match or permit the projection, or else there is discord.

Since it is claimed that production of ambivalent form or influence by individual alternative permits relatively undetermined thought to take place in individual observer (as opposed to action on the part of individual alternative determining thought in individual observer), if there is discord between the projection of individual alternative and field, the relatively undetermined thought permitted on the part of individual observer will be disorderly—nothing wrong in an absolute sense perhaps, but timing and demands of social dictate will not be furthered.

The ambivalent form has not the same communicability or interpretivity as action. Action can be read. Actions are self-evident, especially with the development of the individual. It is certainly fair to observe that an adult sees much more in a social scene that a child sees.

There is a certain circularity involved in the notion of projection, and ambivalent form production, on the part of an individual alternative serving as an undifferentiated basis for undetermined thought on the part of individual observer. The projection of individual alternative depends upon what that individual senses in the environment. To what extent is this solely dependent on individual alternative?

If the environment includes a natural phenomenon, or purely impersonal events, perhaps projection is different from when other individuals are in evidence or in relation to the individual alternative. Consider if the individual observer is prominent to the individual alternative, occupying a focus in his / her environment; might not the ambivalent form production of individual observer him / herself affect the individual alternative sensorily? This would result in projection in individual alternative and a subsequent production of ambivalent form by the individual alternative, which, it is proposed is a basis for undetermined thought in individual observer. If this is so, then the individual observer has influenced his own thought capacity by means of his ambivalent form production in the presence of the individual alternative.

This is the distancing necessary, when the problem of an individual's control over their own thought processes could not be resolved, due to a contradiction of thought affecting thought, of thinker affecting thinker.

Instead of a thinker affecting thinker bootstraps type of a consideration, one dwells upon the thinker as an influencer, and socially as a self-influencer.

Then, instead of the dilemma, how to control or affect thought (by means of thought or determination), one can pay attention to the ambivalent form production of the self, and desist, if possible, from this ambivalent form production, or attempt to maintain awareness of every ambivalent form by adherence to origination.

Production of ambivalent form corresponds with influence or the eliciting of a unit of consciousness in a target individual. That is, that opposite of the ambivalent form is not considered so much a content of consciousness, but actually a unit of consciousness.

The ambivalent form may be part of visual experience; examples are facial features or environmental arrangements visually perceived.

However, the ambivalent form ought to be no less easily imaginable as audible, audial arrangements of environmental stimuli (and perhaps all senses contribute in this way). It may be that the audial ambivalent form is as important if not more important than the visual ambivalent form.

The ambivalent form primarily elicits the conscious opposites, and / or is combined with other ambivalent form to make projection. However, ambivalent form production also results in another "oppositional association", that when an action is elicited instead of consciousness, i.e., idea as intent is evoked.

To state action is elicited is contradictory, as so far action has been considered as an originating process: that is, not or never a reaction. The view arises at all due to a perception that ambivalent form produced by the individual may "give away" the intimate condition of the source – this would be due to an arising in the target individual of the same type of an association as occurs in infancy and which is at the basis of the individual's understanding or mastery of intent as an aspect of interrelations. In that infantile condition nature permits and the environment facilitates a co-origination involving nascent individuals, while they are fully accessible, ambivalent formally or perceptually, to one another.

Disclosing or giving away the individual's intimate condition (intent, motivation or emotional tone) may be possible if the alternative individual or incidental target finds an origination corresponding with the ambivalent form production of the source or individual observer. This is basically the same as that process which pertained more constantly during infancy, but then was meant for the development of a capacity to assign and recognize intent.

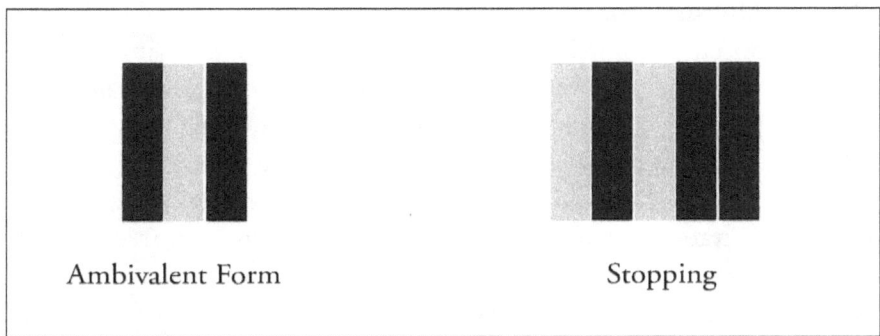

Figure 21.

The figure above shows not action, but action's opposite; "stopping" as it is termed, or beginning or ending. One has not compromised the originating nature of action since one invokes not action but it's opposite, stopping, which nevertheless implies action.

With gesture as action, the interindividual relations are either a) order with individual alternative <-> idea with individual observer (and this describes the knowing of action, or actions being readable); there is a communicability inherent in action. However not, or never, order with individual observer (see Figure 22), or b) a power <-> restriction interrelation, as with individual observer with power, individual alternative with restriction, or vice versa. This implies action as an accomplishment even in spite of the other individual.

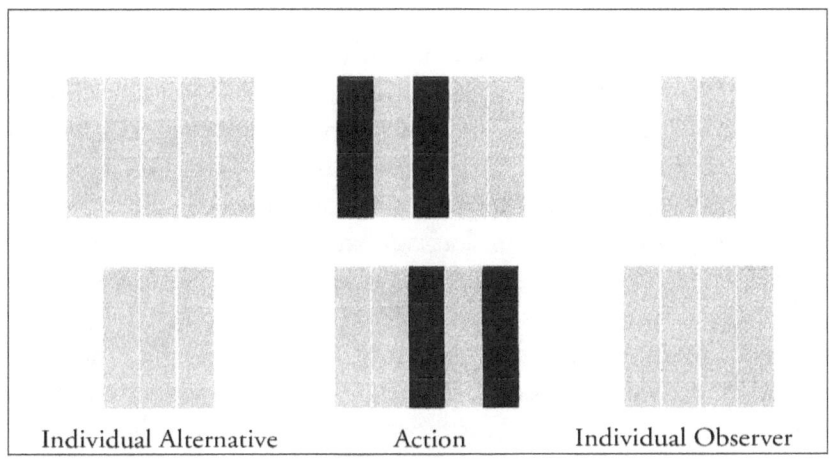

Figure 22.

With ambivalent form, one refers to what is pre-gestural. It is not a matter of conscious knowing (involving idea), but of eliciting a unit of consciousness in the opposing individual. With a word "ambivalent" one seeks to imply that though the influence is present, it is not guaranteed that the unit of consciousness will be elicited in the opposing individual; that depends on the condition of the target—past learning and experience. Once the elicitation occurs, the ambivalent form is captured and this results in an alteration in the ambivalent form. The ambivalent form is subsequently "on" as opposed to its previous off or neutral state. This is the on-off potentiality that leads to the application of the term ambivalent to the form.

The interindividual relations for ambivalent form production are order with individual alternative and power with individual observer.

Figure 23.

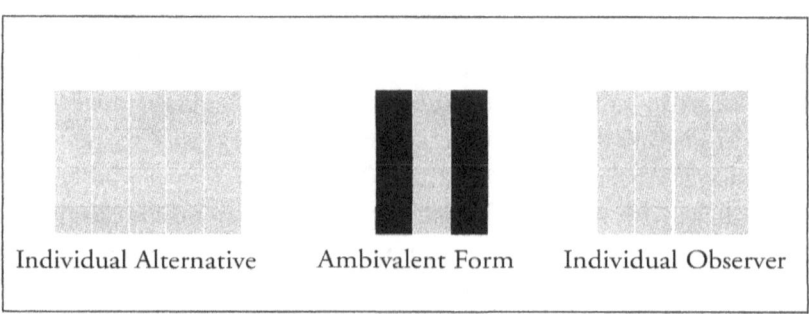

Individual Alternative   Ambivalent Form   Individual Observer

Where does this power come from? It belongs to the self-exterior and derives from a contraction-like occurrence of the self upon its interior, and which occurrence excludes the four single primaries (see Figure 18). These can then be imagined as adhering to the self-exterior. The application of the power is forced when a uniting process leads to a loss of the exterior. It is suggested that this is something that can happen ten times a minute—that is, it is not such an extraordinary process as might be thought. If this process really does occur, it is frequent and a matter of development.

Influence requires this ambivalent form production. If an individual is not visible, one must make noise, or perhaps, if one is perfectly settled and silent, one releases chemicals, odors, or whatever may be influencing.

IN SUMMARY:

a) Influences are not determining. Action is a "determining influence", but that expression is not used, as it is a contradiction in terms.

b) The interindividual relations restriction <-> power is the condition when action occurs. Power on the one individual's part implies restriction on the others; action necessitates a social dominance. For the majority of cases this is trivial. Also, if it were known, adherence to a restrictional condition by the one individual may facilitate action on the part of others—perhaps a sort of creative-thought condition (restriction).

c) Comparison of boundary, real and movement, and that something that is not movement, yet not stillness (ambivalent form) and which can be an important intermediary socially and psychologically; is made in terms of the two principles (primary and secondary).

d) Order is posited as always on the alternative individual's side of the relations, and power on the observer's side. Influence depends on an identity of the alternative individual.

e) Field, and what society permits in the way of influence, can only deter the production of the ambivalent form, not forbid. How deterring and formative is field is not stated. Self-influence, the root of self-control as it lies in one's own ambivalent form production in the presence of others, is also subject to the opposition between field and projection. What one permits oneself to think is socially bound by field.

APPENDIX

REGARDING THE IMAGE patterns, or primary / secondary schemata used, e.g. action or idea formation; if it is questioned how one can justifiably claim these descriptions as valid, in answer it is stated: the urge to try such descriptive schemata followed one year of prolonged daily exposure to the I Ching. Absorbed in the work, insight occurred in direct association with certain of the patterns or hexagrams (which are based on a dual yang-yin system). For example, Hexagram 48, The Well; Hexagram 52, Keeping Still; and Hexagram 11, Peace. Eventually, the recognition of nearly every hexagram involved some strong association(s). (When I said hexagram I meant I would throw the three coins, six separate times. Since then, I have not used the I Ching. However, the drawings are almost always of the maximum five lines that have been used in this paper).

The system using five instead of six lines, which is here put forward, is simpler, especially since only some of the thirty-two (2 to the power of 5) possibilities are considered.

There is a new book out, written by a Chinese-American physicist, Kerson Huang. Essentially it is a new translation (or interpretation) of The Book of Changes. Whereas the Wilhelm / Baynes translation is one dominated by the philosophy of Confucius, one can assume some sort of a strong reaction to Confucius in China this century, and this has influenced the new version, which claims to be more of a popular version.

What this writer has learned of Confucius from Wilhelm's version has led to a great admiration for the old sage.

However, the physicist, Kerson Huang certainly represents modern Chinese culture. He indicates that the Book of Changes is revered in his family, a little as the bible is in western society.

Some of his interpretations are interesting, complementing what Wilhelm wrote in sometimes disturbing, sometimes enlightening fashion. There certainly are some things that could be said about a comparison of the two versions.

Kerson Huang was a friend of Chen Yang while they were both at Princeton. Yang had by then collaborated with another man Tsung Dao Lee of Columbia University, and in a paper of 1956 (and in other papers perhaps) proposed that nature is not left-right symmetric (to do with the weak interactions of particle physics). An experiment in 1956 involving neutrinos verified their predictions, and Yang and Lee received the Nobel Prize in 1957.

This is an instance of where one would have to be knowledgeable of physics and chemistry to understand the interpretations (of natural symmetry).

Huang himself, very objective, dismisses any turning of science towards the inner, subjective life of mankind. One could hardly argue with him.

However, from the I Ching and western philosophy together, hopefully some new thinking could emerge, new and stimulating for a westerner anyway.

The descriptions of this paper, though they are not very convincingly or strongly developed, may be a pre-scientific attempt.

As an example of how the definitions arise, consider action, which is complex and hard to describe. Part of the justification for settling on this schema for action derives from the I Ching hexagram 48, The Well, which is like action, except for the presence of an extra secondary at the bottom as in Figure a.

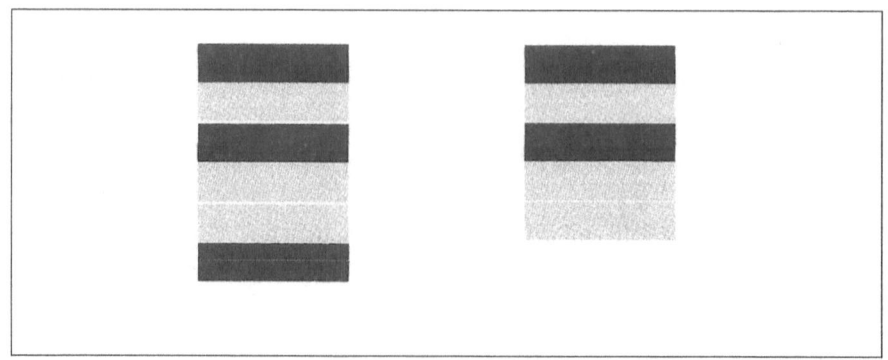

Figure a.

That The Well, despite all the metaphor and anecdote of the I Ching's text, refers to the inner state of being and origination was assumed. Also, field or "what is right" is also mentioned in the relevant commentaries for this hexagram.

JAMES P. DEVANEY

ACKNOWLEDGMENTS

I Ching, by Kerson and Rosemary Huang, Workman Publishing, New York, 1985, 1987

I Ching, The Chinese Book of Changes, Wilhelm / Baynes translators, The Bollingen Series, Princeton University Press, 1967

The Bhagavad Gita, Maharishi Mahesh Yogi

"The Origin of Language: Aspects of the Discussion from Condillac to Wundt", by G. A. Wells, 1987, Open Court Publishing Company, La Salle, Illinois

The bases of social power, Raven / French, 1959

Visual Perception, Tom Cornsweet, Academic Press, 1970